Aunt !
May you be
closer to Him
than ever
before !

Come Worship
the Lord

love you
Angel

COME WORSHIP
THE LORD

Abba's Daughters Ministries

ANGEL

Pleasant W rd

Pleasant Word (a division of WinePress Publishing, PO Box 428, Enumclaw, WA 98022) functions only as book publisher. As such, the ultimate design, content, editorial accuracy, and views expressed or implied in this work are those of the author.

The author of this book has waived the publisher's suggested editing and proof reading services. As such, the author is responsible for any errors found in this finished product.

Unless otherwise noted, all Scriptures are taken from the *Holy Bible, New International Version*®, NIV®. Copyright © 1973, 1978, 1984 by the International Bible Society. Used by permission of Zondervan. All rights reserved.

Scripture references marked KJV are taken from the *King James Version* of the Bible.

Scripture references marked NASB are taken from the *New American Standard Bible*, © 1960, 1963, 1968, 1971, 1972, 1973, 1975, 1977 by The Lockman Foundation. Used by permission.

ISBN 13: 978-1-4141-1327-2
ISBN 10: 1-4141-1327-7
Library of Congress Catalog Card Number: 2008910631

Are you content with your physical,
mental & spiritual content?
Is your glass half full?
Do you complain about what life has and is
dealing you?
Is your glass half empty?

"Do You Know Who You Are?"

"Do You Know Whose You Are?"

Abba's Daughters – Daughters Of God

Adopted – Chosen, Hand Picked

Called For A Purpose

My daughter, before you were even formed in your mother's womb, I knew you. I know the thoughts and plans that I think towards you, thoughts of peace and not of evil, to give you a future and a hope. Call upon me, come pray to me and I will listen. As you seek me, you will find me if you look with your whole heart. You see, my precious daughter, I love you with an everlasting love and draw you to me with my loving kindness. Just for you, I gave my only son, Jesus, that you could choose through Him eternal life. Come daughter, dwell in the secret place with me, draw near and I will draw near to you. I will impart to you things that you can share with yours sisters that you all may be encouraged. You are and forever will be my precious and special child. I love you!

Abba Father
I want to thank you for the precious gift you
have given us in Jesus. I want to thank you for
your Word that we can glean understanding
from it; and come to know you more.
Teach us, Father, how you feel about us. Teach us
to draw near to you that you may draw near to us.
Holy Spirit, come. Guide us. Reveal to us this love
that the Father has for us. Not that we love Him,
but that we love Him because FIRST
He Loved Us!
Father help us to know how you feel about us, not
just read about it. Help us to walk securely, fully
knowing that we can bring our sisters to birth into
our beautiful family. Thanks you, Father.
In Jesus Name
Amen

CONTENTS

Precious Sister, Daughter of God

THIS BOOK IS dedicated to our Lord and Savior, Jesus Christ, and to the Holy Spirit who would have us, sisters and brothers alike, draw near to the Father in Spirit and in Truth. It is all about relationship. It is all about intimacy. My prayer is that you would receive revelation as you read through this and as you act on it, may an overwhelmingly awesome thing happen in your relationship with Abba.

In an attempt to get my attention, the Holy Spirit took me to my knees in prayer for days to teach me more about relationship; more about intimacy and more about Abba. It was an awesome experience for me, and I would like to share what I learned with you. Remember, it is a choice thing. It is all about how far you are willing; how far you will choose to go with your relationship with the Lord. You will never be forced but there is always an open invitation for you to COME.

I wonder if we are truly surrendered to our Father in heaven. Do we really comprehend the fact that the Holy Spirit wants to flow through us like a river in worship unto the Father… worshipping Him in Spirit and in truth. Jesus is the only way yet do we understand who Jesus is? Sure, He died on a cross for us but what about His example of relationship on the earth? Do we just want the savior, or do we want to have and be all Jesus offers to us to the glory of the Father?

Are we truly the worshipful church we are called to be? Are we a church that spends endless amounts of time and energy on the activities that make us look like a church or are we a body of believers that can be seen of men to know our God intimately?

"Oh, God… we cry out to have our questions answered yet still you give the same reply…"

"My child, I have answered and shown you. *I love you with an everlasting love and draw you with my loving kindness. (Jeremiah 31:3)* Come to me."

"We cry out, O God, from deep within to worship you. Our desire is to be united to you, to hear your voice; to see your face look on us. We desire to know you intimately enough that when we come together in one accord and in one place; we all will truly be the worshippers you have called us to be. O, Father, you are Spirit and we desire to worship you in spirit and in truth.

We love to love you, O Lord, our God. We love to love you and draw nearer. When we come to seek your face, we find mercy and grace.

Oh Lord! To be yielded to you; to sing of the love we have for you; oh, how we cry out to you… Your presence falls over us and our arms reach out to be held by you. Only you, Lord, can come and hold us without ever picking up the ugliness that we've held from the world; and now it just falls away. Hold us, Father! Like a child when picked up by their daddy, we go limp in your presence; falling to our knees yet we are also being held lovingly in YOUR arms."

Our Father wants us to want to be with Him; to choose Him. He will never force Himself on us but He constantly invites us to draw nearer. Once we make the choice, He woos us to a place nearer to Him, a place of glory. Oh, the glory of His presence! This place changes as we draw nearer and He will only allow us as far as we are willing to go. This place is like a date and we control what can and cannot happen. The things I will share with you, my sister, are in comparison to an earthly loving relationship.

In a relationship you might have with a boyfriend you set limitations, and you do this with God. As a boyfriend wants more and more, so will God desire this of you. You, also, will want and expect more in that relationship. A real relationship requires effort. If both parties don't put forth that effort the relationship will not grow. If effort is put forth the relationship thrives and is seen by others bringing forth a desire in others to have what you have.

When you are with a special someone you just want to be close to them. Nothing else matters around you because your attention is on them and theirs is on you. God is a jealous God and He wants our attention. He also wants to give His attention to us in ways that we experience and know it is Him. There can be a place with Him where you feel like everything could fall off... cares of this world fall off, gone... clothing, jewelry, make-up and things suddenly find themselves worthless; of no value because He wants you and sees you as you and all of these other things are just things. Draw near and He will draw near to you...

"Father God, how wonderful it is to be here with you. How awesome it is to be in your presence and know that it is just you and me. We cry out to be united with you as one like the prayer Jesus prayed in John 17. There seems to be no care here except to please you. This place of glory where nothing can be taken away; where we have chosen to be in your presence and everything but You has become meaningless. You, Father, have brought me to this place and shown me that I am special to you and that you love me. I feel it! I know it like never before. There is a freedom here where all the weights of the world have been lifted off and we are strengthened to our feet as though we float upward as a feather in the wind. This freedom makes our arms lift upward to You. Our bodies flow in a dance that feels as natural as... Is the place where you want us—here-- Is this worship? Sharing and enjoying one another's company in such an intimate way? Who could imagine such a thing with our maker? Draw me closer, Father."

How can I explain except to proclaim to you, my sisters, and to all people that we must seek the face of our God. We must unite with Him in a place where He can speak to us and love us. My prayer is that you will receive revelation knowledge in your relationship with Him and that you will use wisdom in applying this knowledge to experience something you never imagined before. There are no words to explain what He has for you... no words, except He Bids You Come To Him!

Worship Unto the Lord

I WANT TO get right to the point with you about worship. I want to share words of songs that you may or may not have heard before. I want you to understand that this is scripture and it is powerful to read. It is powerful to apply to your life. It is powerful to pray; and it is powerful to sing…

There is power, power, wonder working power in the…

Mmmm, you know this, don't you? It is all about Jesus and what He has given you before, at and after the cross. It is all about how much of Jesus you want in your life. *John 1* tells us many things that we tend to read over but when we read it we need to ask God to reveal to us more about Jesus.

Have you ever had a best friend? Have you ever had a best friend whom you trusted introduce you to a guy that they claimed might rock your world? Well, Jesus is that friend and He wants to introduce you to His Father and further you in a relationship that is going to rock your world.

I have shared with you about being Abba's daughter, Daddy's little girl. This was to bring you to an understanding of who you are in Christ and how special you are. This book will bring you into the knowledge of God as your friend and companion; the lover of your soul. We have relationships with many people and to gain understanding about our relationship with God we compare to our earthly relationships BUT THERE IS ONLY ONE GOD. Since there is only one God, our relationship comparisons, IF WE GROW, will also change and grow. In this booklet, we are looking for an intimate adult type of relationship with our creator; our God.

Let me ask you something. Can you get into worship? Singing to the Lord? When you hear a song on the radio about God, (1) do you sing just to be singing along because it has pretty words or a nice beat –OR- (2) does it stop you in your tracks and do you sense a need to sing to God? If you answer #1, then I suggest you prayerfully consider #2 examining yourself and question God why you don't feel this. Your relationship should always be growing and you may not be here yet but you can be. God is real and wants a real relationship with you.

2

If your answer is #2, then we need to continue on. When you stop and sing to God, have you sensed the Holy Spirit direct you to a place where you sense God is pleased and wants more time with you? Call on Him...

Abba Father Abba Father Mark 14:36
Deep within my heart I cry
                                    —Mark 14:36

Abba Father Abba Father
I will never cease to love you
                                    —Romans 8:15

Abba Father Abba Father
Deep within my heart I cry
Abba Father Abba Father
I will never cease to love you
                                    —Galatians 4:6

Sing over and over, these words that bring pleasure to Him, and find yourself in this place I call worship. Notice the words you are singing are no longer about Him but to Him. Sometimes we never realize that there is a difference in these words we sing. Wait on Him!

1- Beautiful Isn't He
Isn't He Beautiful
Prince of Peace
Almighty God
Isn't He... Isn't He... Isn't He...

2- Beautiful, aren't you God
God you are beautiful
Prince of Peace
Almighty God
Yes you are… Yes you are… Yes you are…

Do you see the difference? The first one is about Him, and in corporate worship; these words are telling listeners about God and draw us, and others, into His presence. The second one is to Him. It is all about telling Him what you think of Him and drawing near to Him. It can be used in corporate worship or in your alone time with Him, but we must remember that these are more than mere words when it comes to relationship.

Imagine a boyfriend saying something to you that was just words that really meant nothing to him when saying them but you thought it meant something when you heard them spoken. Words are precious and powerful whether spoken or sung and this is one reason we hear the scripture so often telling us to be slow to speak and quick to listen. In James, we are reminded that there is the power of life and death in the tongue.

Again, imagine a boyfriend hearing you speak about him, praising him, to someone else. It blesses him and in this, he desires to bless you in return. You and I may not even realize why the blessing has come our way, but suddenly it has and our praise about him becomes praise to him. This is as it should be in our relationship with Abba.

So, let me ask you again; can you get into worship? Have you experienced worship? Can you picture Him as you worship? A smile starts to appear at the corner of His lips... continue on... continue on... When we worship Him, we bring pleasure to Him; yet so often we quit too soon leaving Him dry. We quit because we are just giving lip service and have not come to the place of yielding our hearts to Him. Heart service is worship.

Have you ever been in a relationship where your partner stops something before you wanted to stop? How did you feel? Did your sudden negative vibes stir a negative reaction? Imagine being in a place where you are pleasing God then the phone rings and you just drop the moment running for the phone, then come back. What happened? You lost the moment.

Psalm 149:3, 4 Let them praise His name in a dance: let them sing praises to Him with the timbrel and harp. For the Lord takes pleasure in His people: He will beautify the meek with salvation.

We are told that His people perish for lack of knowledge in *Hosea 4:6*. Continue to worship Him and know that He has gotten full pleasure from your pure worship. He is Spirit and we are to worship Him in spirit and in truth. He wants to reveal things to us in this time we spend with Him. Relationships are not developed by writing information about someone down or receiving information about someone as someone else perceives. Relationships are developed through spending time with another and getting to know them; building a trust and an understanding of what their make up is. It is also opening yourself up in this relationship to allow the other party to get to know the real you. God wants this from us and it will require time and effort. We can learn lots about Him from others but we can only know Him and His desire for us individually if we seek Him for ourselves.

Welcome the Holy Spirit into your place of worship. He is like a chaperone giving direction and nudges when needed. He is a gentleman and never forceful so invite Him to be a part of your worship experience. You will be surprised at how much help He will be to you. Remember to be honest and real in this worship experience. Worship from the heart not just from the mind. *John 4:23 tells us to worship in spirit and in truth.*

Sing to the Lord
a New Song...

God, you are Wonderful
Wonderful aren't you, God
Prince of Peace
Almighty God
Yes you are... yes you are... yes you are...

God I want to worship you
To worship you is what I want
To draw near
Forever more
You're my God... You're my God... You're my God...

ANYTHING IS POSSIBLE when you draw near to Him in worship. Words stir inside you and you will find them rolling off your tongue and through your lips. When you spend time with a special someone, you are drawn to them and a desire wells up in you that stirs the heart and mind to do something special for them and to say special words. You find yourself doing things you never imagined you could do thus the scripture that says to us that we can do all things through Christ who gives us strength. Come, worship.

Do you have a need? Is there a desire in you that has gone unfulfilled for a very long time? Are you lonely? Do you drive yourself to unnecessary levels trying to meet the expectations of others; and even worse the unrealistic expectations of yourself? Is there just that ever lingering thought that something is missing in your life? If you answered "yes" to any of these questions; I pray you would draw near to Him and experience this place of worship. If you answered "no" to all of the questions, I pray that God would raise up some people to pray for you and minister to you so that you, too, would come to a time in your life desiring to worship our heavenly Father through worship.

Reach out and touch the hem of His garment; and receive as did the woman with the issue of blood in *Luke 8:43-48*. There is always an open invitation for you to come to Him but He does not force Himself on you. He will meet you where you are so when you come to Him, it will not be the same as when I come to Him. Your and my desire is not the same. Our willingness to draw near is not to the same place; and our willingness to open ourselves up can not be equaled. You must choose for yourself. Once you start the journey to draw near in this relationship, a new choice will have to be made each step of the way.

It is as though you accept the opportunity to go out on a blind date. When you arrive to the meeting place, will you choose to join the date or walk away? Will you sit and talk or will you allow your mind to wander? Will you participate in a second date? Oh my dear sister, would you walk towards this opportunity presented to you? Would you touch the hem of his garment and see what He has for you?

In pure worship there is power available to you that you cannot imagine. It is a power that only your faith can control and only your faith can allow you to go. The hem of His garment is a possible place of beginning but you can choose more. You can choose to grab hold of His hand...

Walk with Him, and He with you.
Talk with Him, and He with you.
Know that you are His.

Some might take this opportunity to sit on His lap and hold Him to them. To feel His embrace comforting you is like no other feeling you can know. You might remember a time where someone special held you to comfort you just out of love but maybe during a time of need. You cannot imagine experiencing this with God for it is far greater than your best experience. Come, and worship Him.

There is no greater joy than to be in this place with Abba Father; for He will reward them that diligently seek Him. *(Exodus 15:26 & Hebrews 11:6)* You can find Him in this place of worship. Sing to Him... Receive from Him; healing, love, joy, peace, comfort... through the Holy Spirit, worship the Father in spirit and in truth with your heart and mind.

Praise Father, Son and Holy Ghost
Praise Father, Son and Holy Ghost
Praise Father, Son...
Praise Father, Son...
Praise Father, Son and Holy Ghost

Songs may come to your mind that you know or have heard that cause a stirring in you to draw nearer; maybe sing louder. The words may change or some new words added but don't stop and please do not be fearful of it not being good enough. God hears your hearts cry.

Praise Father, Son and Holy Ghost
Praise Father, Son and Holy Ghost
Praise Father, Son...
Praise Father, Son...
Praise Father, Son and Holy Ghost
Sing hallelujah to the Lord
Sing hallelujah to the Lord
Sing hallelujah
Sing hallelujah
Sing hallelujah to the Lord

He is the Lord that healeth thee
He is the Lord that healeth me
Peace has come for your soul
Rise and be made whole
He is the Lord that healeth thee...
—*Exodus 15:36*

COME NOW,
AND PRAISE HIM

WORSHIP HIM. LET the desire well up in you and follow through. Let the river of His love flow freely that it might overflow allowing you to experience some thing you have only dreamed about. Tell Him how you feel. Tell Him about the love you have for Him. Tell Him you want to draw nearer than ever before. He will not move away from you as some people might, afraid of this closeness. Draw near to Him and he will draw near to you. His desire is for you; for us, to draw near but He waits on us to choose. With every nearing we draw to him, He draws nearer still to us. Exalt Him.

I exalt thee
I exalt thee
I exalt thee, O Lord...

Talk to Him. Tell Him how you feel about what He has done for you through Jesus... the cross... the resurrection... He loves you so much and loves to hear that you recognize this. He loves for you to share how His love and power touched you through His giving His only Son for YOU... for His only Son walking this earth as an example for YOU... for His only Son giving His life for YOU, yet that you recognize that His Son Jesus didn't stop there but that He still lives for YOU that you might choose life through Him... that you might follow His example and draw near in the same type of relationship with Him because You are His child also. You are His pride and joy and His rewards in this relationship can be far greater than any reward man could give... far greater than any reward you can give yourself... He has shown you how much He loves you and invited you to draw close to Him and He waits. Will you come? Draw Near. Worship Him.

I exalt you, O Lord my God
I exalt you, O Lord my God
And worship at your footstool
I worship at your footstool
For worthy are you
Worthy are you...
—Psalm 99:5

I love you, Lord
And I lift my voice
To worship you
O, my soul, rejoice

Take joy my king
In what you hear
Let it be a sweet, sweet sound
In your ear…

There are songs we have heard. There are songs we think we know. There are songs we can and have experienced. Worship Him.

Yes, I exalt thee
I exalt thee
I exalt thee, O Lord
I exalt thee
I exalt thee
I exalt thee, O Lord…
For thou, O Lord, art high
Above all the earth
Thou art exalted far above all gods
For thou, O Lord, art high
Above all the earth
Thou art exalted far above all gods…

Sing in the spirit and if new words come, let them flow freely from within you for God has given you a new song. Sing it unto Him for you are the righteousness of God in and through Christ Jesus. The anointing is upon you and His desire has been made known to you and will flow through you as long as you will allow it. You are a blessed gift which gives to Him many gifts including this new song… worship Him.

I rejoice in your salvation
In your truth that never ends
I give thanks for
You've redeemed me
And your mercy endures forever and ever, amen
—Psalm 136

Sing psalms, hymns and spiritual songs to Abba Father. These are all His words given to people and to you to give back to Him in song, word, and in deed. It brings Him pleasure so give it to Him especially during those times you feel so moved to do so. Some might call this the Spirit moving on you. There will also be times when you will have to give a sacrifice of praise. Times when you just don't feel like it BUT if you will draw near; He will draw near to you.

Love Him as you draw near; as you sing… feel His presence. Know that He is actually there with you, holding you, comforting you even where you may think there is no need for comforting… He is there! Worship Him freely. *Freely give and freely you will receive. (Matthew 10:8)*

Lord, make me an instrument
An instrument of worship
I lift up my hands in your name.

Lord, tune me, your instrument
Your instrument of worship
I lift my whole self in your name.

Lord, play now a love song
A love song of worship
I lift up my voice in your name.

Now, Lord, make us a symphony
A symphony of worship
We yield ourselves wholly to you…

So often, in reading this scripture, we think it is talking about money and things BUT I want to share with you that it also is talking about us; the giving of our spirit, soul and body freely to Him. We must yield ourselves to the Father. The more we yield to Him; the closer we allow Him to get to us. As an individual, we each choose how close we will get to Him. We cannot blame nor credit this in our lives to anyone but ourselves. There is no greater joy that we can have except in worship to Him, on this earth. The love and closeness that you can experience is awesome AND as you experience God in this way, you will find yourself applying what you receive to your earthly relationships. It is indeed awesome!

Our God is an awesome God
He reigns from heaven above…

Isn't He Beautiful Beautiful Isn't He
Prince of Peace Almighty God
Isn't He Isn't He Isn't He

God knows your heart

He knows when you just want to sing and sound good to yourself or to a listener. He knows when you want to just be close to Him. He looks at the heart and our reward is received through the intention of our heart and mind. The body just acts out what our hearts stir in our minds.

> *Come; let us return to the Lord*
> *Come; let us return to the Lord*
> *Come; let us return to the Lord...*
> *—Hosea 6:1*

We must come to a place in our relationship with Abba where we can know that in any and every situation, we are to worship Him. There is victory in this place of worship. Satan cannot stay in a place of worship to the Father... he is jealous... he runs because he knows that if you are exalting Abba Father then you are not exalting your problems or happenings in your life and this gives Him no place.

Things in our lives, good or bad, should be shared with God giving Him the glory for He is doing good things in our lives. This draws us nearer to Him and He is in ecstasy. The devil, on the other hand, rejoices when we do not do this because he wants only to draw you away from God and he doesn't care who or what is exalted to do this. People give the devil too much credit and he loves every minute of it. The devil thrives on our choices to give God second place. Now, we know and so Come, and *worship the Father in Spirit and in Truth. John 4:23*

Halleljuah Hallelujah Hallelujah Hallelujah
Halleljuah Hallelujah Hallelujah Hallelujah
Hallelujah Hallelujah

Unto the Lord My Savior
Be glory both now and ever
Glory forever more
Amen Amen Amen

Unto the Lord Almighty
Be glory both now and ever
Glory forever more
Amen Amen Amen

Wow! I love to praise and worship my Father in heaven; and to exalt the name of Jesus whose name is above every other name. You know, Jesus is forever on the throne; forever at the right hand of the Father and nobody nor any thing can ever change that fact. Hallelujah! I love to tell my precious Holy Spirit how much I love Him in a song for He is my helper, guide, reminder and teacher. I love to lift the name of Jesus and to worship My Heavenly Father in Spirit and in Truth and the Spirit leads.

Unto the Lord My Savior
Be glory both now and ever
Glory forever more
Amen Amen Amen

Unto the Lord Almighty
Be glory both now and ever
Glory forever more
Amen Amen Amen

When I sing songs, hymns and spiritual songs in this place of worship; even in the times I find myself quieted, I sense His presence like never before and there is a happiness in me that I cannot explain except to say that I know that my Father has received great pleasure during this time because I give myself to him. I give to Him that which is in my heart and this is pure worship. My heart may cry out with a need or it may be rejoicing in something I have received but either way, I give Him my heart. The way I sound or the way I say or sing something is not my worry because He looks at my heart.

In Philippians 4:6, we read that we are to not worry about anything but pray about everything with thanksgiving in our hearts; we are to make our requests known to God. You see, we can share with friends and relatives what is on our heart or mind but when we share with God, it is another experience altogether; like nothing else. God knows what we do, think and want but He desires that we share with Him these things so that in sharing you might come to know His desire for you.

We can come to a place where we delight ourselves in Him and He will give us the desires of our hearts. When we draw near to Him with our whole heart, His desire becomes our desire. His will shall become our will. He invites us to join Him and we do and the desires He has placed in us become fulfilled. It is amazing.

Our Father
Who Art In Heaven
Hallowed Be Thy Name

Thy Kingdom Come
Thy Will Be Done…

Mix Prayer with Singing

PRAY AND SING the scriptures. You are giving His Word back to Him. Worship Him! You will find a whole new joy in your prayer time. Remember that we are to come to the Father through Jesus. It is first, His Father and He, Jesus, is His only Son. Jesus may a way for us to come as His brother or sister and allowed us to be able to say of God; Father, Abba Father…

> Abba Father
> Abba Father
> Deep within my heart I cry…

Pray His Word to Him. Sing His Word to Him. *Delight yourself in Him and He will give you the desires of your heart. Psalm 37:4*

Dear Father in Heaven:

As the deer pants for the water, O Lord, so my soul longs after you. You alone are my hearts desire and I long to worship you…
—Psalm 42

Create in me a clean heart, O Lord; and renew a right spirit within me. Cast me not away from your presence O Lord, and take not your Holy Spirit from me. Restore unto me the joy of your salvation, and renew a right spirit within me…
—Psalm 51:10 – 12

Lord, you are my shepherd and YOU are all that I want. You make me to lie down in green pastures. You comfort me with your rod and staff. You alone cause me to triumph. Surely your goodness and mercy shall follow me all the days of my life and I will dwell in your house forever and always…
—Psalm 23

In Jesus Name I pray this… amen.

The Lord is so beautiful to me even though I have not actually seen Him with my natural eyes. I want to know Him more and find out how I can please Him more. I know that in doing these things, His eyes are always on me; not because of what I do but because of His love for me and He sees that I want more of Him. Even during those times when I slip up, He has someone there to lift me up whether it be in prayer or through some type of encouragement. His grace abounds to me continually. His hand is on my life even though I cannot see it. I have made this choice to press forward with Him, have you?

When I sing to the Lord, His Word, He knows that I seek after Him and I can easily flow with a song in my prayer language which in song has to be a blessing from the Lord. It is always beautiful, flowing ever so gently and lovingly out from me unto Him.

Your face is all I seek
And when your eyes are on this child
Your grace abounds to me...

If a certain song doesn't come to you, then just sing over and over of your love for Him.

I love you Lord
I love you Lord
I love you Lord
I love you Lord

When it seems that your whole world is crashing in around you, worship Him! This worship is like prayer unto the Father in song, yet it is also a sacrifice of praise. You are giving Him something even though you really do not feel like it, but you will soon find your whole attitude is changed. Exalt your Father in heaven and not your problem. Cast all of your cares on Him for He cares for you.. (1 Peter 5:7) Worship Him and push through till you find yourself worshipping Him with a voice of triumph and victory. Jesus forever reigns in any and every situation. Healing can flow; miracles can happen; peace can overcome you during this time of rejoicing in the Father. Peace and joy can pour into your life and situations as you worship Him with a new song, and the love of the Lord abounds to and through you. It's amazing! Others can see the difference that worship makes in your life. Worship Him! Sing to Him a new song which the Lord shall put in your heart. Many will see and trust you Lord because of this. *Psalm 40:3, 4* The angels will play the music as you rejoice in song unto the Lord. Come now; cast all of your cares on Him for He cares for you. Sing of the mercies of the Lord forever. *Psalm 89:1*

Would you bow down before Him? In this you would be placing Him in higher position than yourself. It is not an easy thing to do if you have not developed a relationship of worship with Him. To bow down, you would exalt Him but you would also reveal to others that you have placed Him above yourself. It will be a witness to all who see you. Would you; could you bow down before Him? Would you kneel before the Father as you worship Him; as the Holy Spirit directs you? *Philippians 2:10*

O come, let us bow down: Let us kneel before the Lord our maker. *Psalm 95:6*

Do not let what others think of you as you worship, hinder you in worshipping our Heavenly Father. Consider the rocks who will cry out if we do not. Let us worship the Father in Spirit and in Truth for it is those who do so whom the Father seeks. *John 4:24*

Exalt the Lord our God
Exalt the Lord our God
And worship at His footstool
And worship at His footstool
For Holy is He… Holy is He…
                              —*Psalm 99:5*

In His presence, we know nothing but the love and goodness of God; and if we stop and look around, we may find that it is just us and Him… or you may find that others have joined in. Imagine God's people joined in worship unto the Father, united in pure worship…

High praises of God within our mouths
The Sword in our hands
                              —*Psalm 149:6*

And one by one we shall become
The kingdom of Christ…
The body of Christ…
United with Christ…

THINK ABOUT AND MEDITATE IN THE WORD OF GOD

TRY PSALM 91:1 – He who dwells in the secret place of the Most High shall abide under the shadow of the Almighty. Make it personal. I, if I dwell in the secret place of the Most High shall abide under the shadow of the Almighty. His Word is for me; for you.

If I, we, dwell in the secret place of the Most High God, we shall abide under, His, The Almighty's shadow. This shadow is like a covering of the Almighty. Imagine the covering a new mama puts around her newborn baby to protect it and then around the blanket, the mother wraps her arms tightly. Consider all the layers of protection that a mother tries to lay out to cover that baby; to protect it. Abiding under the shadow of the Most High can be considered to be like this BUT EVEN MORE SO!

As we worship Him, could this covering be His arms wrapped around us? Could we be united in a type of ecstatic worship that we can not be separated from the Father, not broken apart for anything during this time. Could the world be actually set apart from us and Him as we abide under the shadow of the Almighty? We must learn to come to Him; to worship Him in such a way that we can go into this secret place, to be in His presence. There can be no better place except that we draw nearer still. At this point, we will want only more and more of Him and though we will find times where we feel separated from Him; we can go back to that place as we practice the presence of God in our lives. It can become a natural part of breathing and living. There is none like Him. He says that if we will draw near, so He will do also.

Are you walking in this place of worship? Listen to yourself… The words that you speak will reveal to you and to others where you are with Him. The words that come forth from you will reveal if you trust Him with all of your heart and lean not to your own understanding. It is revealed whether or not if you acknowledge Him in all of your ways. His Word in us is alive and is revealed in and through us. So often we claim to know God yet in reality, we only know of Him. We need to search the scriptures for ourselves. We need to apply them to our lives. We need to develop a relationship with God for ourselves and this becomes a light that shines so brightly from us that others see and desire the same, giving God the glory. *Matthew 5:16*

So, examine yourself and see where you are with Him. Examine the words that come out of you in various situations. Are they uplifting and encouraging; edifying? Do you speak forth the Word of God? You do not have to quote scripture and verse, but the truth is the truth only through the living Word of God. Out of the abundance of the heart the mouth speaks. *Matthew 12:34* If we go on to read in verse 35 we will see that there is a treasure that may be seen of men that reveals good and evil. Worship is a treasure given to us from God to share with others. This treasure is not to exalt ourselves but it is for God to be exalted so we are to take the treasure He gives us and return it to Him as a treasure from us to Him. We need to put forth the good treasure and not the evil. God sees our hearts and so often our hearts are far from what is spoken from our mouths. Though we may say one thing, God knows. If we can truly come to know how to dwell in the secret place of the Most High then we can say of the Lord He is my refuge, and my fortress. He is my God and it is in Him I trust. *Psalm 91:2*

Make it Personal to Him!

TAKE THE WORD of God and apply it to your prayer time and to your worship time with Him. Make it pure worship from your heart to Him. It pleases Him when we take what He gives us and we give it back to Him in a sharing way like this. You can sing to Him.

> *I will say of you Lord*
> *You are my refuge*
> *And my fortress*
> *My God, it's in you I will trust…*

When we dwell in the secret place of the Most High, in that place of worship, we can sing forth and it is like a treasure in us we share with God. We can believe and know that no evil shall befall

us; neither shall any plague come near our dwelling.
Psalm 91:10

Our dwelling is all that we are and all that
we have. Know ye not that you are the temple of
God?

His Word is alive and can be active and evident
in our lives but first we must seek Him through His
Word and through prayer for ourselves. Next, we
must combine the two. How can we know what to
say in prayer, praise or worship if we never learn
what the Word says to us? How can we apply the
Word or know what to do or what to expect if we
never glean from what God has given us in and
through His Word?

In this secret place, no weapon formed against
us shall prosper. This does not mean that no weapon
will form against us. It means it shall not prosper
against us. God gives us opportunity and shelter
but be assured that the devil will offer the same
opportunity and shelter hoping to turn you away
from God. You always have the choice. God will
not force you and the devil cannot force you. Don't
allow yourself to get caught up in a place of excuse
or blame because the bottom line is that it is your
choice. The battle in this world is a spiritual one
and not one against humans but we want so much
to be in control that we leave God on the sidelines
when in actuality the battle is His and He has already
won. The devil knows this and tries desperately to
sway us and when we choose his way; he is exalted
in our lives. When we blame the devil; he is exalted

in our lives. When we run trusting in the name of the Lord, it's like running into a strong tower where we are safe. *Proverbs 18:10*

When we go to the secret place and dwell with the Most High... He takes care of us. The devil cannot go into the secret place with you. The world cannot go with you into the secret place with you. They may still be there waiting but in that secret place God will share things with you for He is your refuge, a fortress about you where no weapon formed against you shall prosper and no tongue will rise up in judgment against you without His permission lest it is condemned. *Isaiah 54:17*

We should fear no evil if we dwell in that secret place. Worship Him in spirit and in truth John4:23, 24 and you will find yourself dwelling in the secret place of the Most High God, and you will abide under the shadow of the Almighty. You are covered by the blood of Jesus. He gave His own life as a sacrifice for you; for each of us. His blood atoning for our sins made a sweet savor to God. This gave you an open door to worship Him; to dwell in that secret place and say of and to the Lord: "YOU ARE MY REFUGE! YOU ARE MY FORTRESS!" and you will believe it! You will trust Him more and more and come to believe all that He reveals to you in and through His Word. You will not fear any evil that shows itself to you trying to scare you because you will know where to run for safety and guidance through because you know that the battle belongs to the Lord. How can we know unless we truly experience God for ourselves?

Come Worship the Lord
For we are His people
The flock that He shepherds
Come Worship The Lord
And bow down before Him
For He is our God

Hallelujah Hallelujah
—Psalm 95:6, 7

God's Word gives direction for our lives but like any directions we must first choose to accept them and then choose to follow them. So often we choose to get directions after we have gotten lost or after we find that something is not exactly right. Again, it is our choice to accept and follow the direction God gives us through His Word. There are two things that are important to point out about God's Word, (1) *God's Word is Jesus John 1:1, 14;* and (2) God gave us Jesus in Word and in a person of example (*John 3:16*) that we might choose this direction for our lives. The Word instructs us to go to the Father and Jesus through example shows us to go to Him, but always as a choice of our own free will.

Where we lack vision and understanding, God has placed teachers before us that we may learn through them but we must have ears to hear. God will not force Himself on us, but He will allow us to choose for ourselves what direction to move in. It is our own choice in whether or not we choose to worship the Lord, to develop and have a close relationship with Him.

If we ask it shall be given to us; seek, we shall find; knock and the door shall be opened to us.

—*Matthew 7:7*

It is our choice to make the first move. The Word also explains in *James 4:2, 3* the reasons we do not receive. First of all, are we seeking/asking? Second, are we asking for the right reasons? Are we asking to draw nearer to God or are we asking to be seen of men for what is given to us? Are we really trusting and believing that He can deliver? On the other hand, could we be wanting more and more from Him yet unwilling to give to or for Him? So many questions and yet we can only examine our own hearts.

Have you given yourself to Him in pure worship? Pure worship from your heart? Don't give excuses to yourself because God knows your heart. He wants you, each of us, to examine ourselves and then come… All things are possible with God (*Matthew 19:26)* and He being able to do anything gives us each the choice on how close we will draw near to Him.

Don't be the one to say "if I cannot have it my way then I am not doing it God's way either," or another way to voice this would be "if God won't do this for me then He better not expect me to do what He wants." Always remember that God knows what is best. He knows the perfect and right way not just the good way. We must learn to adhere to that which the Holy Spirit speaks to our hearts. We do not want to be waiting on the Lord forever, especially if He keeps sending us direction yet we do not listen or follow that direction. We need to be obedient to be true worshippers. We want to receive the fullness of what God has for us.

YOU CAN SEEK AND NOT FIND
YOU CAN KNOW YET NEVER SEE
BUT IF YOU WILL LISTEN TO MY SPIRIT
SAYS THE LORD
YOU WILL SOON FIND ME

This is not a song but a Word given to me one day when I was singing to the Lord. It was a beginning for me in worshipping the Father in Spirit and in Truth.

How Long
Must He Wait?

ACTUALLY, THE ANSWER to this question is up to each individual. He will wait, and believe me when I say that; He will wait because He created patience and is all patience. We may find that in our choosing to turn away from this call to worship that He will allow us to learn more about patience also. A time may come, though, when He must move forward with His plan and you could miss Him with your excuses. Consider the story of Jonah. Please don't put off what the Lord has for you today. Trust and believe in Him. Worship Him in Spirit and in Truth.

Philippians 4:6 tells us to be careful for nothing; meaning not to worry about anything… but by prayer and supplication with thanksgiving in our hearts, let our requests be made known to God. If there is thanksgiving in our hearts then there is love, joy and forgiveness and this will bring forth a song in his presence as we draw near and thus, we find ourselves in this place of worship.

Find your place with the Father
and
move forward in your relationship with Him.

Come Worship the Lord
For we are His people
The flock that He shepherds

Come Worship The Lord
And bow down before Him
For He is our God

Hallelujah Hallelujah
Hallelujah Hallelujah

Worship Him Worship Him Worship Him
I worship You I worship You I worship You

We can sing/talk about Him or we can sing/talk to Him. It is a choice we each make. We can tell people about the experiences others have had with God or we can have experiences with God of our own that we can share. These experiences are testimonies.

In the Old Testament we read about how the people would worship before the Lord, yet now, we are to worship in the Lord. *Rejoice IN the Lord always and again I say rejoice. (Philippians 4:4) Worship the Spirit IN spirit and IN truth. ((John 4:23, 24) God* made a way for us to come to Him for ourselves through His Son. We no longer need to rely on a priest. We no longer have to bring a sacrificial gift to stand before Him. Jesus, in us, opens the ways to draw near yet we must choose to allow this to happen. Jesus is in us yet we are the temple in which He is housed and if the door stays shut; Jesus is hidden away from onlookers as well as from His Father. If you have asked Jesus to be your Lord and Savior then you are forgiven; saved. What's next is a choice we each must make and this is why so many people look at their brother and sister in Christ and say"You are not saved." There is a lack of evidence in their lives that Jesus exists in them but that is between each individual and God.

Will you choose to worship before God or worship in Christ?

When we sing to the Lord, we can be joined to Him as the Holy Spirit dwells in us. We can sing to Him or about Him. There is a difference and we can choose the way we want to worship. We no longer have to wait on a king, priest or prophet to go in before us; or to go in on our behalf. *Jesus has made us kings and priests. (Revelation5:10) We, each, are the temple of the Holy Spirit. (1 Corinthians 3:16, 17) We are a chosen generation, a royal priesthood, a holy nation, a peculiar people that should show forth the praises of Him, who has called us out of darkness into His marvelous light. (1 Peter 2:9)* You can be engulfed by it if you will worship Him in Spirit and in Truth. The worship will become continual inside and outside of you. You can and should be a temple of worship unto the Father CONTINUALLY.

Come into the holy of holies
Enter by the blood of the lamb
Come into His presence with singing
Worship at the throne of God
Lifting holy hands
To the King of kings
O worship
Jesus
O worship
Jesus

We are called to worship the Father according to scripture *John 4:23*. Coming into the holy of holies requires that we must first enter through those gates of decision. This is where so many people are right now. It is a place of feeling comfortable versus moving on with what God wants for them; for each of us. Once we make the choice to come through this present gate of decision; we can draw near to our Heavenly Father into His holy place. We have to choose again and again as to how far we each individually are willing to go with God. His love is forever and always, but His promises are conditional. The more that He sees that you can handle, the more He will allow you to have...according to His Word...

Do you know His Word well enough to receive what He has for you? If we do not know what He has to offer then how can we know what to expect; to strive after?

We can do all things through Christ who gives us strength according to *Philippians 4:13*. If we do not know that this is in our Bible, how can we expect to partake of it; much less walk in the fullness of it? Maybe we know it is there but do we understand what it means? Many think that Christ is Jesus' last name but Christ is the anointing Jesus had walking this earth and that same anointing He has made available to us. To be strengthened to do all things, we must allow the anointing of Jesus to flow through us and to do this is another choice; a gate of decision. It is the same with worship; choose to allow this anointing of Jesus to flow through you to the Father.

Okay, you get through the gate(s) of decision and you come into His presence with singing. Will you continue until the Holy Spirit reveals to you that you are finished and that the Father is well pleased? Will you run to answer the phone or do a load of laundry in the middle of your worship time? Will you refuse to allow the things around you to keep you from drawing closer and finding out what more the Father wants of you; for you? Will you sing; continue to sing until there is a breakthrough? You set the time… the date… the place… how long… The decisions are all yours and He waits…

You have chosen to continue on into yet another new place with the Lord; in His presence with singing. Words begin to flow from your mouth; words from deep within you... from your heart to His. The Father receives your offering and bids you come. Draw near to Him and He will draw near to you. (*James 4:8*)

Now, we must enter through into that presence and become a part of His presence which has been made available to us through the blood of the Lamb. We know that the Lamb is Jesus, our final sacrifice. We know that the only way to the Father is through Jesus for it is written in *John 14:6*. Jesus is holy, powerful and full of all authority which was given to Him by His Father. Nothing can be compared to the blood of Jesus that was shed for us all. (*Matthew 28:18*) When we received Jesus as our Lord and Savior, we also received His cleansing blood that has washed away all of our sins. This blood was shed for you; for each of us, and has made us holy and acceptable unto the Lord. It has made us adopted into the family of God giving us a power of attorney of sorts. This allows us to walk in that same power and authority. It opens the way for us where the way was closed before. It is YOURS and mine IF we will choose to do as the Word leads through the guidance of the Holy Spirit.

The Old Testament tells of the few chosen to go into the Holy Place and death would come to those who were not chosen. Not just anyone could come into the presence of such goodness but Jesus changed all of that for us. There is a new covenant and we are all invited to come into the Holy of Holies except now we cannot come unless we choose to walk in Christ. We must choose to walk in His power and authority and not our own. We must choose to walk in relationship with Him. This is not a part time; want to feel good experience for us to have. It is a commitment and God looks at our hearts not just the words we may think sound good.

God meets us where we are and draws us to where He wants us to be BUT if we stop, He goes no further. He knows our hearts and wants no part of a show. He is looking for a forever, full-time commitment. We can go places that are unimaginable, but first we must trust and believe in Him; trust and believe enough to let Him be in control of our lives.

We enter into this place of worship, becoming as one with the Father, through the blood of the Lamb, Jesus. Sing now, as you are united with the Father. Come to that place where you can find ecstasy. Worship at His throne of grace. He wants you with Him and has provided direction. Fellowship with Him. Reach out and touch Him. Learn and know those places that you can bring the Father great pleasure. This is where He will want to please you in return… in your obedience to Him… and He does know exactly what you need. This is a place of pure worship. Lift your hands in awe to Him! Be with Him. Exalt Him! Let Him know how you feel about Him…

In this time with the Father, you can actually be exalted with Him in a place that is more than ecstasy as we know it. Rejoice in His presence. He desires that we know Him; truly know Him. He wants to but only if we allow Him. He will reveal truth to us in ways that we have never known. He will reveal what we are to do with this truth he shares and then we will choose whether or not to be obedient. He will reveal that a part of our drawing near to Him is in our obedience and He will draw nearer still to us when we choose His way.

Worship Him...

in the fullness thereof... IN spirit and IN truth; In Christ. Don't stop because of time. He holds time in His hands and wants us to understand His timing. Interruptions? God is indeed a jealous God and does not want us to allow anything to interrupt the time we have with Him. Any type of interruption will hinder us in our worship time with Him. Continue in that place of worship; communion with God; fully uniting with Him. God wants us to give ourselves to Him completely... our whole self beginning with our hearts and minds. This worship that we have with Him must be with more than our lips. No lip service will be acceptable to Him. He wants us in our totality. No vain worship. *(Matthew 15:7-9)*

We must freely choose to worship God the Father to the fullness He expects of each one of us individually thus uniting ourselves to Him. *(Exodus 25:2)* He made the way easy for us through

His Son. All we must do is choose to be obedient. Worship is: our offering ourselves to the Father in pureness of heart and mind. Where so many get pleasure in seeing beautiful stones, jewels, abundance of monies and/or things; where so many seek position and title, our Heavenly Father gets pleasure from us seeking Him instead at this same measure and more. This is how we enter into the pure, precious worship He is calling us to. This is worshipping the Father In Spirit And In Truth.

Consider the rich man who came to Jesus exclaiming all he had done and his reaction when Jesus told him to sell all that he had and come follow Him. How can we worship the Father in Spirit and In Truth if the things this world offers is exalted in our lives above the Father?

In the old testament, *Exodus 25 * God gave instructions for a sanctuary to be built so that He could dwell among His people. At this point, the people would worship God with all of their own power and strength yet were never united with Him; never feeling His presence nor hearing His voice for themselves. They had to hear from God through someone else. The Father could only be among them; abide with them. They couldn't handle being in His presence just around His presence.

Today, we have a new covenant

through Jesus and we are the temple of the Holy Ghost. He is in us for we, when accepting Jesus, have

47

become His dwelling place and that same spirit that raised Christ from the dead dwells in us but we do control movement and so we choose to be a type of sanctuary that worships the Father in spirit and in truth or one that does not. We choose to keep Jesus in the small room of our hearts alone or do we allow Him to worship the Father through us; and at what measure do we allow… We are the sanctuary where worship flows from. We no longer need the building except to fellowship and for corporate worship with other believers/worshippers. We are a place of worship to the Father in spirit and in truth. We are to be doers of the Word and not hearers of it only according to *James 1:22*. What kind of dwelling place you are is due to the choices you make. God has opened a huge doorway inviting you to enter into His presence and He waits for you…

I will call upon the Lord
For He is worthy to be praised
So shall I be saved from my enemies…
—Psalm 18:3

The Lord liveth
Blessed be the Rock
Blessed be the Rock of my salvation…
—Psalm 18:46

What type of dwelling place are you, will you choose to be? Where is your place of worship? The plans are written out for you by the master designer and now we each choose whether or not we want to use these particular set of blue prints or if we want to make changes to suit ourselves which could weaken the foundations of the dwelling place.

We can read through *Exodus 25* about the plans in building the tabernacle unto God. This place was a sanctuary where God would abide, dwell, and where those men given authority could go and speak with God. That is where the faith of the people was at that time. Only those who had proper authority could get a word from God and only those same men could speak in behalf of the people to God. The people waited on this chosen one to hear from God for fear of dying in the presence of such goodness, holiness and purity.

It is so very different today and God has opened a way for us that so many still do not know or understand. It seems unimaginable to me to have to wait on someone else to tell me what God wants of me; how I should act or believe and to not recognize Jesus in me and the power He has made available to me in obedience to the Father. I cannot imagine not being able to worship Him nor to dwell outside of His presence. God gave us a perfect gift in His Son Jesus but the gift is not just a package we open for salvation but it is a gift that keeps on giving revealing more and more of itself as we seek deeper within the package.

Consider the people who wait until every Sunday to hear a message from their pastor about God. God wants to speak to each of us and He wants us to know Him personally and not just know about Him. He wants us to know Him every minute of every day; to share ourselves and our lives with Him. When we do not understand then we have pastors and teachers to guide us.

On Sunday morning look around at the people who have come to "so-called" worship. How many of them bring their own Bible? How many have their Bible open when the preacher speaks? If they do not bring their own Bible, can you expect them to open a Bible at home? Think about it. Many people wait for pastors, preachers, priests and teachers to tell them some great revelation of God; or to teach them secret antidotes that will enhance their lives. We are each invited to seek God through His Word ourselves and this is a part of a growing relationship with Him. God wants to reveal Himself to each of us individually. The more we seek, I seek… the closer we/I can become to Him. This is what makes His Word come alive in our lives. This is what makes those secret antidotes really evident and working in our lives. In *Matthew 6:33* we are told to seek first the kingdom of God and His righteousness and then all of these things will be added unto us. Take a few moments right now and open your Bible up to *Matthew 6* and read it. See what God has for you in it…

Read about the workmanship and the beauty of the Old Testament tabernacle and all that is to be in it… (Beginning in Exodus 25)

it may seem so beautiful, but we must remember that it is a *thing* of beauty. Pictures have been created to show us its beauty, but we need to get past the beauty that we look at in awe with our physical eye. The talents and gifts that are placed in and around the temple of God can at times put us in awe. We must look past these things and look at Jesus. Know that we each are a temple of God that if looked at with the physical eye can put another in awe of us but we want to see Jesus; and we want others to see Jesus in, through and around us. The things seen of us are added blessings God shares with us but the ultimate blessing is Jesus and He points us to the Father above saying, "Worship Him in Spirit and in Truth." It is Jesus who opens our eyes to see but it is a choice we each make with what we will do with what He shares with us. In all things around us, Jesus is there. Will we see Him? Can we know Him? Do we allow others to see Him or to see us? Who will we glorify? My prayer is that we will see Jesus and get to know Him in such a way that others will see Jesus in us also.

Many times, unknowingly, we are watching each other, making a judgment not understanding that we each are called according to His purpose and although the plan unfolds revealing the good and the evil in our lives; God knows the outcome. Who are we to hinder His plan because we cannot see past the present? We watch and judge others yet do not examine ourselves. Before we know it, we wonder why we can or cannot do what another is doing; or get what they get; or why can't they be like us. We get stuck in a rut of watching what we think is the beauty or ugliness of another temple of God. When we do this, we do not consider the temple we represent and what is happening to it. God, our heavenly Father, is looking for purity of heart. We should be forgetting those things which are behind, and reaching forth to the things which are ahead; pressing toward the mark of the high calling of God in Christ Jesus through us. *(Philippians 3:13, 14)*

We are all called, but few chosen

ACTUALLY, TO ME, I read this to say that all people are called yet few chose to listen to the guidance of our most precious Holy Spirit, which means that someone has missed their call. It doesn't mean God doesn't get His way because He will place a call on someone else. His will, His timing and His callings will be fulfilled with or without us. We must learn to keep our focus on Jesus and not the situations and/or circumstances around us. Don't have your eyes so attached to the people and the things around you that you miss Jesus. Even the Word tells us that the traditions of men make God's Word of no effect. We just need to understand that those traditions make the Word of no effect in the life of the one who chooses that way. What if there is no tomorrow? Will we be caught up in building and rebuilding a physical building calling it God's temple or will we be amongst the temple itself, the body of Christ; rising up doing what we are called to do. Worship the Father in Spirit and in Truth. Let us get caught up in uniting the temple to worship; teaching and drawing others through our example letting our light so shine that others see and glorify God. Let us follow Jesus and not just follow men who say they follow Jesus.

Please understand that God has given us pastors, teachers and such to help give us direction and to instruct us to seek God's face but they are not the way for us to get to the Father. Jesus is the only way and we cannot move forward in our relationship with God through someone else's experiences and relationship. Although we all do not hold titles we are all called to bring others into the kingdom. When they are in, who will teach them to carry on; to overcome? These things that I speak to you about, now, are for those that are already a part of the body of Christ. We need to grow in the Lord, not just sit back and wait on others to do it for us. You are the temple of God, living or dying, and this is of your own making and only you can examine yourself to determine the truth of what is happening in your temple. The Jesus in you is the same Jesus who is in me and the spiritual gifts in me are available to you. It's all about Jesus and when we accepted Him, we accepted all of Him so He is here but at what measure we each allow Him to operate in our lives personally; each of us individually.

What am I saying? Jesus is the same yesterday, today and forever… unchanging. The change comes in the choices we make. We choose to move forward with God's plan as He invites us to join Him; or we choose to sit and watch as His plan moves forward without us; or we choose to fall back in our sins claiming to be something we are not and unknowingly being a fake recognized by onlookers. We must be doers and not hearers only; but it is our choice. Choose today to move forward in the things God is calling you to. When He calls us, he will equip us. Trust Him. Reach out and not only touch His garment but be a part of His garment, the robe of righteousness that He has provided for you. He bids you come and worship the Father in Spirit and in Truth. Let Jesus and the Holy Spirit do all of the building and rebuilding of the temple. They know better than we do on how to make a strong tower where the righteous can run and be safe. They know the needs of the people and they know exactly what the Father wants. The Jesus in each of us cries out to be in worship unto the Father. Be with Him. The Jesus in each of us, being a part of the three person godhead, wants us united with the trinity. How do I know this? It is revealed in the prayer Jesus prayed in John 17. He, they, want to share with us in this place of pure ecstasy in worship… but, we first, must choose.

Praise the Lord with us! God is good! My first book **"Daddy's Little Girl"** was officially published December 2008, and now before 2009 is half through **"Come Worship The Lord"** & **"Christian Acronym Devotions"** are published and available to order. God is good!

A Call To Pray
Ask, an answer will come
Seek, and you shall find
Knock, and the door will open

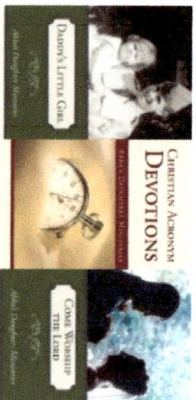

If you so desire, these books are available on Amazon.com, BarnesandNoble.com or straight from the publisher:
~In the top right hand corner, type in the book title you want to see, read about or purchase~
https://www.winepressbooks.com/product.asp?pid=1999&search=2&select=browser&ss=1

A Call To Pray
A day hemmed in prayer is less likely to unravel.

You may be able to order through a local bookstore but being they are so new, they may not be available there yet. It takes a little longer for stores to get them. We wanted everyone to share in our excitement and praise to God in the publication of Angel's books.   *Love Ya in Jesus, Robert & Angel Fulkerson*

Abba's Daughters Ministries   http://home.comcast.net/~abbasdaughters/

God is so good!

H E IS WAITING patiently for you and for me. He will meet us where we are and draw us to where He wants us to be. He will woo us to that place that is right for us individually and we will say repeatedly, "There is no high like the Most High!"

This experience will reveal to us in greater measure an understanding of *Philippians 4:8* where we are told to think on things that are true and honest, things that are lovely and of a good report, things of virtue and things that are praiseworthy. If this would be our focus, our lives... our mindset would change drastically. Others would see an evident change and want what we have. What would we do then? Point them to Jesus!

Give God the glory in all things! Worship Him knowing that He is the giver of life, love and goodness. Anything that is not of a good report is not of God but let us not confuse His correcting us as bad. He will correct those whom He loves so do not despise correction. *(Proverbs 3:11)* If we refuse to act in His correction the consequence may seem grim but He provided a way for a good report and so often we choose not His way but understand that He can work all things for His good. All things are possible for Him so remember that He is a God who gives second chances. It is as though you will always have an opportunity to retake a test you fail.

Receive the correction of the Lord

(Proverbs 3:12)

Understand that sin is nothing more than separation from God. He sees all sin the same; as something that separates each individual from Him. We tend to measure some sin as being worse than others but not God. He sees it all the same and calls us to repentance which is that we should choose to recognize that we have sinned; confess the sin to God and ask forgiveness then leave the sin and seek God to help keep you from returning to that sin. If we take our eyes off of Him and His help here, surely we will return to the sin and once again be separated from God. One of the biggest hindrances here is self worship where we think we can deal with our sin ourselves but we fall short every time. Fix your eyes on Jesus as He bids you come draw near to the Father and worship Him in Spirit and in Truth.

Come, worship Him, trust Him… It takes effort to correct someone and so if He has corrected you it is because He loves you and wants only the very best for you. Sin always has consequence but God will make a way where you thought there was no way. He can make good what we see as a bad situation. Don't dwell in a place of doubt and unbelief; and especially NOT in a place where love is lacking or unforgiveness strives. These things are not of God! The world would make you feel guilty and try to shame you into change but God would convict your heart to help you see a need for change to make things better for you for Him.

Come now, all of you who are heavy ladened; says Jesus in *Matthew 11:28-30*. He offers rest to the weary and suggests that we take His yoke and learn of Him… First, we learn of Him and then we come to know Him and He will always point us to the Father above. This is where we find rest for our souls because Jesus tells us that His yoke is easy and His burden light.

Come worship the Father

COME TO KNOW that there truly is a secret place of the Most High. Come; lie in the comfort of His pleasurable presence. Come, no run, to the strong tower where the righteous know to come and know they are safe. This is a good place to be; a good place to know you can come and be with Him. This place is where you give Him all your cares and He gives you peace… and more. It is a good thing to be with Him and to worship Him… Hallelujah! Glory to God in the Highest!

Worthy O Worthy are you Lord
Worthy to be thanked and praised
And worshipped and adored

Worthy O worthy are you Lord
Worthy to be thanked and praised
And worshipped and adored

Singing Hallelujah

Glory to the King
You are more than a conqueror
You are Lord of everything…

Is the Lord worthy of your praise and worship? Of course He is! The real question is "will you give Him the praise and worship He is worthy of?" I have to say that I will try but there are times I get my back up and try hard not to; but even during those times, I do know He is worthy.

Do you give Him thanks? For what? Everything! Even though it takes time for us to realize it, the only reason we have anything at all is because of Him. We should give thanks. So often, we give something to someone and when they are not thankful, it is hurtful or upsetting to us. Imagine not giving thanks to God for the good things He gives to us.

Do you adore Him? Show Him adoration? When someone or something means a lot to us… when someone or something is dear or special to us… we show adoration towards it which is an outward expression revealing how we feel about it and others see this expression making them wonder, "why?" When we show adoration, others want to know more; they inquire of us and when we share with them, a deeper expression of our adoration is revealed. Do we show adoration towards our God? Do others see and want to know more about Him from our point of view?

Do you speak with Him, or to Him? The difference is whether we tell Him what we are going to do versus our conversing with Him and hearing His voice; learning and desiring His will. Do you listen to Him and obey His requests of you? Do you think He doesn't speak to you? Oh, but He does in His sweet subtle way nudging you and me in the direction He would have us go.

God Forth
in the Name of Jesus!

THERE IS SO much more than we can ever imagine in having a real relationship with Him. There is always more to learn and areas to grow. There is always an opportunity to draw nearer to Him. We are called to study to show ourselves approved *(1 Timothy 2:15)* and this approval comes in our learning more about Him and His desire for His people through the testimonies of others. We each must find out for ourselves what the Word of God is telling us to do. The Word made Flesh is Jesus! *(John 1:14)* Whatever Jesus has spoken is the Word, and we are invited to be obedient to it. Jesus is unchanging; the same yesterday, today and forever. *(Hebrews 13:8)* We change, sometimes with the winds of circumstance and God will never force us but His Word is ever present and we are continually invited to be obedient to its fullness.

Being that we struggle so in being obedient, Jesus gave us a comforter, a helper whom is the Holy Spirit. He is here to help us, but is a gentleman and will not force our will. If we choose God's way and struggle; He will assist us upon request. The Holy Spirit does so very much as a third person in the godhead but He is specifically, according to the Word, meant to **guide** us into all truth. The truth being the Word of God and so we seek and find and seek more to find more… Make sense?! He is also there to **teach** us, to **reveal** things to us (in God's time, not ours), and my favorite is that He brings all things to our **remembrance**. This particular one gives us understanding of the importance of reading God's Word even though it seems like a particular part may be boring or inapplicable to our present circumstance. If we will seek God's Word at all times, an answer through His Word will come to us at the most unexpected time because the Holy Spirit brings it to out remembrance. How amazing!

LET THE HOLY SPIRIT
WORK IN YOUR LIFE

IT WILL AMAZE you. Listen to the guidance He gives you. Receive comfort He sends your way. Know that where we lack knowledge and understanding, He will open a river of what we need so that we can do what the Father desires of us. Some may say that He is not for today, BUT HE IS! Some may say that He was only alive for us in the stories of Acts but I tell you the truth, HE IS HERE TODAY FOR YOU AND FOR ME! Again, I tell you that we are given a choice to accept the invitation God gives us to allow to Holy Spirit to be an active part of our lives. He is an important part of the trinity and He desires to be a part of our relationship. He desires to be a part of whatever is pleasing to the Father. We choose now whether to acknowledge and accept Him or not. Listen and He will speak to you and when He does, listen. He will guide you and teach you. He will reveal things to you and bring things to your remembrance. The more you yield to His being active in your life; the more He will do through you. He will love and speak things through you that will amaze you. He will give direction that will change lives; yours and others.

His guidance has to start somewhere and so I would suggest in your quiet time with God and later on maybe in your corporate worship time. How can you know? His instructions would be like gently sensing a need to do things like:

- lift your hands unto the Father while you are praying or singing songs. Listen to the Words and make them personal words from you to Him. You may feel or sense this desire to lift your hands and think it is silly and refuse to do it and so why would you get further guidance if you do not follow through on one small suggestion sent your way. It is always a choice, your choice.
- whisper "thank you Jesus"
- tell of your love for the Lord to someone else, maybe a stranger. Share a testimony with someone who may be struggling. In you choosing to follow through, you may help another person to seek God concerning their life. In choosing not, well, again I suggest to you that the Holy Spirit will not

give you further instruction. We are called to be faithful to the little things first.

- shout Hallelujah! I struggle with this one sometimes because I really would rather be a quiet worshipper but I usually give in when I know that the Holy Spirit is nudging me. The exciting thing about the Holy Spirit is that He will give you extra chances during a time span to do a thing always giving that gentle invitational nudge. He is trying to help you do things that draw you closer to the Father as an individual in your relationship with Him.
- Bow down before the Father.
- Hug your neighbor and say that you love them; and that Jesus loves them and thinks they are special.
- clean a spill in another room that just happened
- follow someone who just ran out and show them compassion.
- Sing and celebrate in His presence
- Worship the Father in Spirit and in Truth

Do as the Holy Spirit instructs you and know that you are being obedient to the Father and Jesus also... You will be blessed and others seeing will also be blessed through your obedience. Your obedience becomes a teaching through your example and not just mere words that are spoken in command. You reveal that an invitation was given to you and you enjoy being obedient. No one enjoys having demands placed upon them but to be invited to join God in what He is doing is a blessing to enjoy and to watch. It is the Word of God revealed through action. It is letting your light so shine before men that they see your good works and GLORIFY OUR FATHER IN HEAVEN. Hallelujah! People will want to know about and be a part of His goodness. They will want to know how they can hear His invitations for them to join Him. They will see you and question you; and you will teach them and point them in the direction of the Father and He will begin a relationship with them that is personal and what they are called to. We each are called to an individual and personal relationship with God and so we cannot expect the same things thus we examine ourselves and seek God concerning ourselves and we grow. It is like being a tree that bears fruit and new shoots making new trees but they, too, will grow and produce fruit… Where you were learning and opening up to be taught; you become a teacher where others can come, learn and dwell in the awesome presence and goodness of God.

Let's talk more about
this process

First, SOMEONE MUST yield themselves becoming like a wide open vessel waiting to be filled with something. This someone must be determined because surely there will be some things that happen that may cause them to struggle like a vessel that may get a chip in it. The world would take that chipped vessel and set it aside BUT GOD WOULD STILL USE IT IF IT STILL WERE OPEN TO BE FILLED. Follow the instructions given you and you will see great results and these results will be your blessings. Hearing the testimony of others will motivate you and excite you but having your own experiences and your own testimonies will bring pleasure beyond what you can imagine.

Come learn of Him. Draw near and worship Him in Spirit and in truth. Don't be fearful of what may happen or of who may be watching. Know that God is in control and trust Him. God has not given you a spirit of fear but of love, power and a sound mind. Look forward to that which God will do in and through you. Be confident that He has started a good work in you and is faithful to complete it. *(Philippians 1:6)*

Jesus is now highly exalted by God the Father, and is given a name which is above all names. A time will come when every knee will bow and every tongue will confess that Jesus is Lord, to the glory of God the Father. *(Philippians 2:9-11)* It is a good thing to give thanks unto the Lord. *(Psalm92:1)* Worship Him *(John 4:23, 24)* in spirit and in truth. Bow before Him. *(Psalm 95:6)* Proclaim that Jesus is Lord! Don't wait until that day comes when everyone will be forced, or you may miss it altogether. Choose this day whom you will serve. *(Joshua 24:15)*

Hosanna… Hosanna…

Hosanna… In the highest…

Hosanna… Hosanna…

Hosanna… In the highest…

Hosanna… Hosanna…

Hosanna… In the highest…

(Matthew 21:9)

Hosanna… Hosanna…

Hosanna… In the highest…

Quietly now, wait in the presence of the Lord as the Holy Spirit leads... follow His direction... listen...

*

*

*

Don't give up... don't leave... don't allow yourself to be interrupted... you are in the presence of the Lord.

Wait quietly. Listen...

*

*

*

He wants to savor the moment with you. He wants to enjoy this time of quiet with you and He wants you to enjoy this time with Him. Wait. He will give you direction. He does want to speak with you and for you to speak with Him.

*

*

*

Be still and know that I am God: I will be exalted among the heathen; I will be exalted in the earth.
—*Psalm 46:10*

*Know ye that the Lord He is God: It is He that hath
made us, and not ourselves; we are His people, and
the sheep of His pasture.*
—Psalm 100:3

*
*
*

The Lord will be exalted. Don't keep your
thoughts on the things and circumstances of this
world making them idols in your life; exalting them
above God the Father. *(Isaiah 2:10-18)*

Worship is not necessarily singing words unto
the Lord; it is so much more. It can be singing but
it is actions taken place by you towards God. It is
like an intimacy between a husband and a wife, only
more so, because the Father want us to come to a
place where there is a constant flow continually. He
wants us in a place in our relationship where we walk
with Him and talk with Him about everything. As I
have said so many times before, listen. Relationships
require a two sided communication where we speak
with one another and listen to one another. We
cannot expect a relationship to grow if we speak
at the other nor if we only listen to ourselves. We
must come to know one another and the Holy Spirit
will guide you through. He knows what the Father
desires of you every minute of every day and He will
help bring you through. The Father knows your
heart and your mind but He wants to hear you share

it with Him. Seek Him. Spend Time with Him. Bow down before the Father; giving yourself totally to Him. Sing of your love for Him, but to Him… Make it more than a song. Be still and know who He is… to you. He loves to hear you whisper sweet words of praise and adoration to Him. He is with you. Do as the Spirit leads you.

As you sit being still; think about who He is to you. If I were to ask you at a quiet moment, "who is God," How would you respond? What would you say? You could only share with me who He is to you. Would you say, "He is my God and Savior?" Could it be that you have come to know Him as Friend and Advocate, even Teacher… Only you can respond to who He is to you. You can learn words that you hear others say in explaining God, but the truth is in your heart when you are still in His presence and coming to know Him because in this place He will become more to you as you allow Him to.

There are times to wait quietly on the Lord, for He wants to speak to you… to love you… to instruct you… to bless you… yet, it can only happen through your obedience so when you choose to allow Him to move in your life, you open doors of invitation that are unimaginable. This time of quiet is your time of worship. Feel the warmth of His presence. Know that His love encompasses you. Be sure to listen, for He will speak to you. When you come to a place knowing that He is there; you will know if you should stand ever so quietly in His presence, waiting; or if another instruction will be given. He will overpower you with an unexplainable love; a peace that surpasses all understanding; and a surety that there is nothing as good as being united to the awesome and powerful Most High God. Don't deny yourself this! Don't deny Him this, for this will quench the Spirit of God. He is very sensitive and will not stay where He is not wanted. The guidance and instruction He has given to you up to this point will immediately stop. The Holy Spirit comes to you ever so lovingly, touching your life in ways that only you can allow and in ways that only you are sensitive to. HE WILL NEVER FORCE HIMSELF ON YOU.

The Holy Spirit, at your request, will give to you a little at a time; never more than you can handle yet still uncovering God's glory to you each time a little more than the last. Revelation and understanding will come to you only as you seek Him and are obedient to what He shares with you. It will not be handed to you just through a person telling you how they got it but through your own experiences in prayer, study and worship. Again, I express to you that this means that in your obedience to Him, you will receive further instruction. When you stop; the Holy Spirit can go no further. Remember that He is our comforter… but, He can only comfort us as far as we allow Him to give comfort. We each have that choice.

In Luke 6:38, we read: Give and it shall be given unto you; pressed down, shaken together, and running over, shall men give unto your bosom. For with the same measure that you mete withal it shall be measured to you again.

Don't you think that God could give even a greater measure to man than what man could possibly give? At what measure we give of ourselves to God, He will give even more of Himself to us. What does that say about your and my relationship with God? We must examine ourselves. *(2 Corinthians 13:5)* God has given us each other upon this earth and we can learn from one another by being examples of giving; not just of things but the giving of oneself truly to God. He loves all of us the same as we read in *John 3:16* and He reminds us through His Word that He is no respecter of persons in *Romans 2:11.* He invites us all to come to Him and allows us to come in what measure we are comfortable with. God is always with us and someone is always watching us. Our example of giving to and receiving from God is revealed in and through how we can give and receive of man. Our relationship with God is revealed through our relationships with people. When we learn and trust that God is our provider… When we learn that all that we have is actually God's entrusted to us… When we learn that we cannot put a limit on God; these truths will be revealed through our daily actions and activities.

A relationship cannot grow when there are limitations. Limitations cause a growth stunt whether it is a relationship with God or with a person. When we place a limit then it limits us from going any further. It does not limit the other person in the relationship because they can go on in another relationship without hindrances. All things are possible with God so please do not get caught up in putting limits on Him. He can do anything but He will not force us nor will He give us more than we can handle. The Word tells us that our traditions cause God's Word to be null and void; our traditions make limitations which cause a growth stunt. May we come to a place where we can allow God to move freely in our lives as we draw nearer to Him learning to truly worship Him in spirit and in truth?

Worship God our Father in the fullness of the Holy Spirit's direction, leading and call on your life. The more obedient you are, the stronger the call will seem and the more provision you will see established. If God calls you, He will equip you. Go with the flow of the Spirit. Please listen to what the Lord is calling you to do. We all have a place, and in our walking in the place He calls us to as well as allowing others to walk in their calling; we walk united to do the will of God. In this He is pleased and will draw us closer inviting us to join Him in more of what He is doing. It is awesome to be in His will.

It can be so easy to fall into a trap of trying to tell others what to do and what God is calling them to but still, each of us has a place and a choice. We must teach others but be about the business God has called us to so that we grow with Him. We cannot all do everything and that is why the body of Christ is made up of many members; each equally important. Some may pastor; evangelize; council; clean up after others; teach… The list goes on and on but we must remember that God has called us each to a particular place and if we try to make a teacher into a yard care taker we could have a mess. We do not have to do it like someone else does but we do each individually need to do it as God would have us do it. Oh the blessings that can flow...

When we do our calling as God calls us,

We make up the Body of Christ and the combination of our doing as God calls us together makes it perfectly as God desires. Can you imagine a body having extra parts here and there and lacking parts in other areas? There becomes a struggle and that is why God has a plan that He wants us to join Him in doing. Listen to the guidance and direction of the Holy Spirit.

When we are not listening, results can be obtained as in the days of Noah and the ark. Even though God promised not to flood the earth again; people perish in their disobedience blaming others or situations but the fact remains that each one of us in our disobedience suffers a consequence. In the days of Noah, the people were given a warning as well as direction but they chose not to heed it. Warnings and direction are given continually today; yet still so many choose to ignore it. The worst part is that others follow this disobedience and many suffer who didn't need to. Please follow the direction of the Holy Spirit. Don't get caught up in that temporary "feel good" feeling that can lead you and others astray. Be still, listen and know the presence of God. Obey Him! Is He calling you to find some quiet time with Him? Worship Him in Spirit and in Truth!

Majesty Kingdom Authority
Unto Jesus
Be all glory, honor and praise
Majesty Kingdom Authority
Flow from His throne
Unto His own
His anthem raise
So exalt
Lift up on high
The name of Jesus
Magnify
Come glorify
The name of the King
Majesty Kingdom Authority
Jesus who died
Now glorified
King of all kings…

In the midst of this quiet time in worship, being in His presence; He may request something of you. He may want you to sing Him a love song; and then, come again to that place of quiet. Listen carefully and obey the direction given to you by our precious Holy Spirit for it is in our obedience that we are given further instruction. If we choose NOT to listen, we will receive no further instruction, no direction. God will not give us more than we can handle. He will not force himself on us, on anyone. We must choose how far we will go with Him… in Him. For in Him we live and move and have our being… (Acts 17:28)

Be still and Know I Am God
Psalm 46:10

Choose now to listen and obey the beckoning of the Holy Spirit. He bids you come unto Him that He might direct you towards the Father through Jesus. Paul tells us to not grieve the Holy Spirit. *(Ephesians 4:30)* Can you imagine the body of Christ coming together in worship to the Father; in unity; in agreement; in one accord listening as the Holy Spirit leads? The word "agreement" in the New Testament Greek means "symphony," so imagine the body of Christ being a symphony unto the Father. Don't be unwise, but be understanding in that which is the perfect will of God. Be not drunk with wine, wherein in excess; but be filled with the Spirit. *(Ephesians 5:17, 18)*

Think about the last time you gave all of those things around you up just to sing to the Lord; things including answering the phone, running errands, watching your favorite television show, etc.. When was the last time you experience His presence? When was the last time you felt His love engulf you; that is, if you have ever felt that at all? Did you choose to go on through the next gate of decision… or… did you decide to answer that telephone? You and I always make that final choice.

You can be so overcome by the Lord's touch that it is compared to having an excess of wine, but I am telling you that it is far better an experience and far more fulfilling and without the hangover. To be drunk in the Spirit is a place of worship where you are consumed in ecstasy with the presence of the Lord. HE IS! There is no other way to explain it… HE IS! In *Exodus 3:14*, God said, *"I AM THAT I AM."* It is because of what Jesus has done and is doing for us that we can truly experience the great I AM.

We are told in *Ephesians 5:19, 20* to speak to ourselves in psalms, hymns and spiritual songs, singing and making melody in our hearts to the Lord; giving thanks always for all things unto God the Father in the name of our Lord Jesus Christ. Continuing through verse 21, we are to submit ourselves one to another in the fear/reverence of God. In meditating on this scripture we can further understand the possibility of God wanting us to pray without ceasing. *(1 Thessalonians 5:17)*

One must understand that the same Jesus that is in you is also in me. He is the same yesterday, today and always. *(Hebrews 13:8)* The same precious Holy Spirit that is leading your heart is also leading my heart, and when He gives you or I direction, His expectation is that we will follow. At the same time as we follow His direction, He may speak to yet another with further instruction thus bringing unity in worship unto the Father and this brings Him much pleasure. When we are all together singing unto the Lord, we are all spoken to but we each must respond individually, choosing whether we will listen and obey or not.

Let's say that we have five people together in a room worshipping the Lord; singing a song of love to Him…

I love you Lord
And I lift my voice
To worship you
Oh my soul rejoice
Take joy my king
In what you hear
Let me be a
Sweet, sweet sound in your ear…

The five people sing this song over and over unto the Lord. Could you imagine the confusion if the five people, in the same room, were to sing five different songs, at the same time, in the same place? Start with unity, singing the same song together. Sing until the Spirit of God begins to move and instruct you each to do otherwise. He will know how to coordinate the beautiful symphony that will bring pleasure to God and to you. It may be that all five people will sing five different songs but the Holy Spirit knows exactly what needs to be done to make this beautiful as though each person is an instrument of worship.

One person may be instructed to become quiet; lift their hands up unto the Father. Maybe soon thereafter all will be instructed to do the same. You may notice that one person keeps singing with the same tune but the words have changes; or even a new language is brought forth to the tune of the song you started out with. Two may join that one singing a new song in English. This could be an interpretation or just words of love being expressed from God through them and back to Him again. One person may kneel down and another may bow down. One person may dance and another lay on the floor in silence. As long as each one obeys the instruction of the Holy Spirit, more instruction will be given.

As someone begins to flow in a dance, still singing with uplifted arms, instruction is given all around that room and outside of that room. All of these people are not necessarily doing the same things, but they are in pure worship unto the Father; in unity as the Spirit is directing; thus pleasing the Father above. This time of worship we can give to God is more than what is happening inside that room, but it is touching the heart of God which touches the entire universe. We cannot truly imagine what our obedience to God is going to do for His glory and pleasure. When we please Him, we soon find ourselves united to Him engulfed by the love and ecstasy He receives and gives us by our being obedient. Hallelujah! Glory to God!

This unity, this pure worship, can go on for a long time, if we will listen, obey and trust the Father. The cares of this world can so easily be taken care of by Him while we are in this secret place. This place is where we come to be with Him; where we cast our cares on Him and allow Him to take care of it. There are times when we just do not want to let it go, much less admit to problems or fault; and this will hinder us in our time of worship. God sees and knows the heart of man; my and your heart. He wants only that we would give ourselves, in whole, to Him. This would mean being honest with Him and giving Him the opportunity to reveal what He can do in our lives if we will worship Him and not our situations.

The Holy Spirit can and will lead you, us, into this beautiful place of worship but we choose how far we will go. It is as though we are led to a room and as we enter the doorway we see things that are so enticing yet so scary. We must choose whether or not to enter in. If we choose to enter we see and smell even more; are offered even more. It will be another choice and another choice with each step we take entering further in but with the Father we experience Him through this beautiful exotic worship. The godhead, the trinity, will lead us and touch us and we choose each step as we follow...

Pure worship is beautiful and brings great pleasure to our God. This pleasure is so wonderful that He wants to make us happy also and so being that He knows what would truly bring us joy, He shares with us things of Him that can at times feel like we are experiencing an overwhelming ecstasy throughout our being. In this place we receive revelation knowledge of His Word as well as wisdom to apply it to our lives. When we listen and obey, we fall into agreement with God Himself. We become a working member of His Body which is in action throughout the world; throughout the universe. The acting Body is functioning according to the Head, which is Jesus Christ. Oh the pleasure He receives here! Can you imagine being a part of this symphony of worship He has invited you to be a part of? This intended union of worship… perfected by Him as He desires it…

Then someone new enters this place, picks up a guitar and starts playing a secular song; something that they think is cool and would make them look good to the rest of the group. The anointing has left. The Holy Spirit moves aside. Someone has chosen to place a person or themselves above God. It is important that we keep our focus on God and follow the leading of the Holy Spirit. Strive to keep the interruptions from swaying you away from this place of worship. It's sad to say but we can so easily be distracted away from the things of God assuming that we are still with Him just because we are around other Christians. God has something for you here but only as you continue to draw near. God really wants the very best for you. We can call the Holy Spirit back and have the anointing restored by gently correcting this new arrival and instructing them as the Holy Spirit leads…

I am in awe of His Glorious Presence!

HALLELJUAH! THIS SECRET place He calls us to is like no other place and I pray that many will come to learn to draw near to Him here in this place.

> *I beseech you brethren, by the mercies of God;*
> *that you present your bodies a living sacrifice,*
> *holy and acceptable unto God, which is your*
> *reasonable service. And be not conformed to*
> *this world: but be ye transformed by the*
> *renewing of your mind that you may prove*
> *what is good and acceptable and the*
> *perfect will of God.*
> *—Romans 12:1, 2*

We tend not to worship the Father when our bodies are sick or weak, when our lives are full of turmoil and struggle; but this is when we should really draw near in worship. During our well and blessed times we should be experiencing God in ways that we would know that during the hard times there is a place to run for the Lord is our strong tower where we run and can feel safe. He wants us to give ourselves totally to Him so that when He calls; we answer. We should not allow ourselves to fall into the trap of using caller ID in our relationship with God; seeing that it is He who is calling and figuring we can call back later when we feel like it, we do not answer. Although there are times we will suffer, God wants us to know that if we come to Him, He can make the suffering or the struggle easier to bare. We are reminded that Jesus bore our sicknesses and diseases. *(1 Peter 2:24)* By His stripes we were healed. Sickness and disease are mere words with very in-depth meanings. We see disease and think of it a more serious sickness. Sickness can be of mind, body and spirit as can disease. Consider DIS---EASE... Father God wants to and has made a way for us to be whole and perfect for His own pleasure. He is pleased when we are comfortable. In this place of pure worship, there is healing complete! When we become united to Him, our bodies, our minds and spirits become immediately as He created. It is and was done, finished!

Worship the Father in Spirit and in Truth!

B E THAT LIVING sacrifice to God, a temple of worship unto the Father, uniting with the Father. Don't do as the world does, but do as the Word of God instructs. The Word was made flesh and dwelt among us full of grace and truth. *(John 1:14)* The Word is God's only begotten Son, Jesus. He came as an example and to teach us the ways in which we should go so that we, too can be examples to the world. Listen and obey the Word! In *James 1:22*, we are instructed to be doers of the Word and not hearers only. We can be led into deeper truths, revelations, and a richer, everlasting place of fellowship and rejoicing. The Holy Spirit will guide you and I if we just ask Him. Know the perfect will of God in your life. Get into His presence… Sit in His presence… Be united with Him… Worship Him in Spirit and in Truth! *(John 4:23, 24)*

In Romans 14:8 Paul writes to us, "For whether we live, we live unto the Lord; and whether we die, we die unto the Lord: whether we live or die, we are the Lord's.

Meditate on this scripture and tell me; since in life and in death we are the Lord's, wouldn't it be far better in life to bring the Father good pleasure, delighting ourselves in Him? Do you really think that we should displease Him just to bring ourselves what we think is pleasure but ultimately is just temporary? Wouldn't it be far better to be united with Him aiming for that place of immeasurable ecstasy rather than denying Him His good and due pleasure in us? We are reminded that it is written that every knee will bow and every tongue will confess that Jesus Christ is Lord. *(Romans 14:11)* This sounds to me like a time will come when we will no longer have any choice. Everyone will do it!

Why wait to be forced to do something that is so wonderful and beautiful? All we have to do is submit, worship Him in Spirit and in Truth. We need the unity. *(Ephesians 4:13)* Every one will give account of Himself to God; every one meaning **You** and **I** and **He** and **She**. *(Romans 14:12)* What will your answer be when asked: When they tried to tell you about worship in me; you walked away; why? When I tried to get close to you, you moved further away; why?

Come Now!
Worship Him In Spirit And In Truth!

Don't concern yourself with the things and the people around you during this time with the Father. Let them be His concern. Keep your focus on Jesus. Allow the Holy Spirit to give you direction and draw near to the Father. *The kingdom of God is not meat and drink; but righteousness, and peace, and joy in the Holy Ghost. (Romans 14:17)*

Arise and sing, ye children of Zion
For the Lord has delivered thee
(Jeremiah 31:6, 7)
Dance and sing, ye children of freedom
For the Lord has delivered thee

I will sing unto the Lord
Sing unto the Lord
Sing unto the Lord

I will dance before my Lord
Dance before my Lord
Dance before my Lord

I will yield unto my Lord
Yield unto my Lord
Yield unto my Lord

United continually to you, my Lord!!

Sing to Him a New Song

THAT HE WILL put into your hearts. Let the worship of your heart be like a love song to Jesus, with Jesus; partnering, uniting with Jesus unto His Father (Our Father) bringing Him pleasure.

*Psalm 149:3-5 *Let them praise His name in a dance: let them sing praises unto Him with the timbrel and harp. For the Lord taketh pleasure in His people: He will beautify the meek with salvation. Let the saints be joyful in glory: let them sing aloud upon their beds.*

*Psalm 150:1 *Praise ye the Lord. Praise God in His sanctuary* (Remember that we each are a sanctuary, temple of God): *Praise Him in the firmament of His power.* (Be united with Him)

Psalm 145:18, 19 *The Lord is nigh unto all them that call upon Him, to all that call upon Him in truth. He will fulfill the desire of them that fear Him: He also will hear their cry, and will save them.

I will say to you again: Hear the Word of the Lord!

John 4:23, 24 *But the hour cometh, and now is, when the true worshippers shall worship the Father in spirit and in truth: for the Father seeketh such to worship Him. God is a Spirit: and they that worship Him must Worship Him in Spirit and in Truth.

Psalm 119:105 *Thy Word is a lamp unto my feet and a light unto my path…

Psalm 134:2 *Lift up your hands in the sanctuary (who is the sanctuary?) *and bless the Lord.*

Don't walk away, but go forward in what the Father has for you. Worship in the fullness He has invited you to be a part of; what He is expecting, and what He desires of you.

2 Samuel 7:5, 6 *The Word of the Lord came unto Nathan the prophet saying: Go and tell thy servant David, thus saith the Lord, shalt thou build me an house to dwell in? Whereas I have not dwelt in any house since that time that I brought my children of Israel out of Egypt, even to this day, but have walked in a tent and in a tabernacle.

Imagine this to be God saying to us that the last person He was able make His abode with, be united with, someone who has yielded themselves as a house to dwell in was Moses. He is waiting on us. Joshua was an eye witness to the account of the Father and Moses coming together. *(Exodus 31:11)*

In the Old Testament, the tabernacle was like a tent that they would carry around with them and when they needed it, they would pitch it. In *Exodus 33:7* *Moses did just this, away from the camp, calling it the tabernacle of the congregation. As we read further through to verse 14, we find that when Moses would go into the tabernacle that the other men would stay outside of their own tents watching as Moses entered in to the tabernacle. A cloudy pillar would come down about him and God would speak with Moses. When the men saw the cloud, they would rise up and worship from afar at the doorways of their own tents. Joshua would go in with Moses to watch, and then after Moses left, Joshua stayed. God says in verse 14, "My presence shall go with thee, and I will give you rest (peace). If we continue reading to verse 20, we'll find that God says that no man can see His face, and live... BUT, not a word was spoken about being united to Him; about hearing from Him; or about loving Him and Him loving us.

It is no different today, where people watch each other in church or what ever place or setting we might find someone in a setting to worship the Father. Don't be the one standing back watching someone else enter into His presence; worshipping from afar. If you are going to watch, then be a Joshua, listening and learning so that you can apply it to your own relationship with God. Watch; and then try it for yourself. Enter into His presence and experience God for yourself. Taste and see that that the Lord is good. To taste you must partake; take something in.

We know that God spoke to and through Moses. We know that Joshua was with him. Joshua did not come out with Moses so what was he doing? We know that God speaks to and through people today; and yes, he can speak to and through you. You and I can experience God for ourselves. Jesus made a way for us but we must choose to take that way. Come now, and worship Him for yourself. Enter into His presence by praising Him… in a song or words or even expressions if that is what the Holy Spirit is leading you to do. Worship Him. Love Him. If you have been taught you can't; know now that YOU CAN! The Word of God is the truth and it says that you can. The Word of God says that it is expected of you. Worship Him in Spirit and in Truth! Read through the Psalms but make them a personal expression of adoration, love, praise and worship from you to the Father above. Be joined to Him in a place of ecstasy. Learn and know His voice. Know His presence and all that He desires of you. Learn and know what He desires for you. Be obedient and be blessed.

Okay, let's go back to *2 Samuel*. God said that He set His people free. Are you His people? Be free! You see, God can set us free but until we choose to receive that freedom, we stay captive in what our mind continues to tell us. God knew that David would choose to be obedient and so, He asked him through the Prophet Nathan: Shalt thou build me a house for me to dwell in? David, will you be that next house I can dwell in; the next man that I can be united with; share myself with? Will you be that willing vessel, yielded so that I can dwell in you and you in me? I want to share so much with you and for you to share willingly of yourself with me; will you be the one? God asked David long ago; and today, God is asking you! It was harder in the days of David yet the choice was there. Today the way has been made easy through Jesus. God asks you now. "Will you be a house I can dwell in?" He wants to do a work in you, dwell within you; and not wait for you to do a work in yourself so that He can hang out on the outside of you like a cross one might wear to claim their Christianity.

In 2 Samuel 7:7 God speaks, in all of the places wherein I have walked with the children of Israel spake I a word with any of the tribes of Israel, whom I commanded to feed my people Israel, saying, why build ye not me a house of cedar.

God wanted a place that was stable and set apart that His people could go and learn of Him. He wanted to have that intimate relationship with His people so much; not just with the priests. His desire was not getting across to us then and even though He made the way wide open for us through His only Son, Jesus; we still struggle with comprehending His desire for us... Even His Word tells us that His people perish for lack of knowledge or even worse, through the traditions of men His Word is of no effect. Where there is no knowledge; there is no understanding, no sharing and no growth. God desires to have a personal relationship with each and every one of us for we are His people; the flock that He shepherds. Even a shepherd knows His flock and even a sheep knows his shepherd well enough to come when he calls.

God chose David. How can I know this? The Word tells us that we love Him because FIRST He loved us. *(1 John 4:19)* Over and over through out the scriptures we read about how God chose someone then invites them to join Him in something He is doing. We wonder how David could be chosen and how he could have such a relationship with God but that is just it; they had a relationship. David knew that sin was something that separated him from God and wouldn't allow that. He confessed his faults and failings AND tried to turn away from them. It was their relationship that kept an open line of communication available. David understood that he needed that repentant heart and he continued on trusting that God forgave him and would work with him. People do not like to give up their fears, much less their possessions. David was chosen to **feed** God's people (which is to teach them) and may not even realize this. He taught by example and that was a part of God's plan. He knew that David would not be perfect but He also knew that David's heart was right. It took God making a shepherd boy, David, into a king to cause the people to watch his example. Today we have much help...Jesus...Holy Spirit...Written Word... If you do find a teacher that will teach you; someone who you can see has a special and personal relationship with the Father... WATCH, LISTEN, LEARN and DO IT YOURSELF. God has so much for you if you will be obedient and trust Him. Don't become the one who stands on the outside looking in on the relationships others have never allowing yourself to grow and get any place with God. He has a whole plan for you if you will only come. Worship Him in Spirit and in Truth.

*2 Samuel 7:18 *After the prophet Nathan had shared all that the Lord had spoken and shown him unto King David, King David went in unto the Lord and said: Who Am I, Lord God? What is my house that thou hast brought me hitherto?*

David did not fully understand what God was asking of him yet he trusted Him and yielded himself to God for His purposes and promises that the prophet Nathan has spoken about. David gave himself fully to God our Father, will you? We may never fully understand but one thing is certain; He will keep His promises. Imagine God Himself telling you ahead of time that He was going to have you dance through your city or town streets naked before Him... When the time comes, will you have a heart for God? Will you be ready to fulfill His will as He reveals it to you? Is your life your own or have you given it to God?

2 Samuel 7:25 *King David says: and now, O Lord God, the word that thou hast spoken concerning thy servant and his house, establish it forever, and do as thou hast said.

Please notice that this is not a one sided agreement, but it is a two way covenant. David not only yielded himself to God our Father completely and unknowingly, but he began to exalt the Lord mentioning God's side of the agreement. (*2 Samuel 7:26-29*)

See the Glory
See the Glory
See the Glory coming down

Praise His Name
Jesus Reigns
See His Glory coming down
See His Glory come down...

Receive the Anointing

ON THE CALLING that the Lord has placed on your life by allowing it to flow out from within you. Pray, sing, praise, dance, write, read… Worship the Father with all that is within you. Get into His presence. Unite with Him and others will see the light of God shining on you for His presence will go with you where ever you go. Let the Father establish Himself in you and in your life, and you will begin to exalt Him…He is worthy…

Worthy O worthy are you Lord
Worthy to be thanked and praised
And worshipped and adored

Sing to Him! Don't worry about what you may sound like. Don't worry about who may be listening.

God sees and hears your heart. Sing to Him. Worship Him.

> *Worthy, you are worthy*
> *King of kings*
> *Lord of Lords*
> *You are worthy*
> *Worthy, you are worthy*
> *King of kings*
> *Lord of lords*
> *I worship you…*

PRAISE HIM!

With your voice lifting words of love, honor and adoration *about* Him; lift up your hands that hang down, palms upward motioning that you are giving yourself to Him to be filled. You are letting Him know that you have made a choice. He has invited you to come to Him and you now want Him to come to you. Draw near to Him and He will draw near to you.

I was once told that when we lift our hands, palms upward in a manner of praise, we allow God to pour in all spiritual blessings. Some may feel led to lift their hands with their fingers pointed, reaching towards heaven suggesting they are trying to grab hold of Him or just to touch Him. Remember that God is looking to give to us as well as receive this praise from us.

You will begin to feel His presence which is always with you. Don't stop yourself, continue as you feel led. Do you feel an unction to speak to Him? Do it! The Father wants to hear what you have to say. Every word and every thought is equally important to Him. He wants you to want Him. He wants you to want to share with Him. Yes, and He wants you to know that He wants you.

This place of praise is like that of a relationship between a man and a woman; their first meeting, getting to know one another, starting to date. Someone knew someone special and made introductions speaking praise; making you want to know more about them. A relationship starts. You get to know that special someone better and better as you talk with them, spend time with them. As you do this, they show an interest in you doing the same things. A real relationship is two sided. It is all *about* the other person. The relationship grows and you want to do more to please one another... It is the same in this place of praise with the Father. Someone has introduced you to Him and the things they say about Him make you want to know more. You start learning more *about* Him and He learns more *about* you as you now are yielding to Him. You now begin the relationship. **PRAISE HIM!**

BLESS HIM!

Your voice is lifted with words of love *unto* the Father. Your hands are lifted high as though you

103

want Him to flood your insides with Himself; as though you want Him to pick you up and hold you closer than ever before. You were introduced. You've gotten to know one another and you know that you want to be together. You want Him to know that you want to be with Him and share special time together. Take some time now to gather yourself in the quietness.

"I love you, Lord. You are so very good to me. I want to be with you forever. I want to please you and for you to give me the things that you know will please me."

The more time you spend together, the more strengthened your relationship becomes and now you have given yourself to Him. You have made a commitment with Him. In His presence, you find yourself in awe. You may feel your knees weaken, but it is good to be here in this place. Go with the Spirit.

Yes, fall to your knees. Oh, the glory of His presence in this place of BLESS. Getting to know one another was wonderful but to give yourself to Him is a much more grand experience that one can only experience. It is a knowing of belonging. You feel accepted and safe.

Just as a man used to fall on his knees in front of a woman to propose marriage to her; you have knelt before your God. The man has proposed lifetime commitment to care, love, protect, and provide for her and in return he wants her to care for and love him. He wanted to be blessed by her presence and for her to be blessed by his presence trusting that through good times and bad they would work it out together.

The proposal of marriage is accepted and the becoming a union has begun. They talk and share, making promises to one another as they draw closer towards becoming as one. As they get to know each other they want to know even more, even the most intimate things. The desire to please and love one another becomes stronger.

This is where you are with the Father in this place of BLESS. Your words and hearts intertwined with God's Word becoming as one knowing, pleasing, serving and loving one another. A passion rises up in you that comes from the heart because you know Him and want to know Him more. No false promises can be made in this place. It is a place of giving and receiving; building to a desire that only wants more of the other, more giving and more receiving…growing. God knows you in this place and only truth prevails. This is real. No one can fake God out pretending to be in His presence. Either you are or you aren't.

In your obedience, you will be blessed in return as you bless Him. This will be the beginning of an overwhelming relationship of true love. This place of BLESS is a courtship, an engagement period. How long will you tarry here? It is totally up to you. Get to know one another. Continually draw closer. Know the way that you are feeling about Him right now is just a small portion of how He feels about you.

You love Him because He loves you first. His love is always of greater measure because He loves you with an everlasting love and draws you with His loving-kindness. He wants to BLESS you. He wants you to want to BLESS Him because in this place it is all about Him. **BLESS Him!**

> I bow my knee
> Before *Your* throne
> I know my life
> Is not my own
> I sing to *You*
> This song of praise
> To bring *You* pleasure, Lord…

*

> I seek the giver
> Not the gift
> My heart's desire
> Is to lift
> *You* high above
> All earthly things
> To bring *You* pleasure, Lord…

WORSHIP HIM!

Your voice is lifted with words of love…

> *I love you Lord*
> *And I lift my voice to worship you*
> *O my soul…*

I exalt you
I exalt you....

At this time, you may find yourself singing in the Spirit. You may be singing words of a song that you have never known before and maybe even in a language you were never taught. The words are like nothing you have known before because there is this feeling with them that you cannot explain. It is like an incense ember stirring into a fire that you know lifts a sweet savor up to the Father reaching in and touching those innermost places. It is good to be here. You hands may lift up to the Father but not like before. This time it is effortless on your part. It's as though they are being lifted for you. You no longer care what you are doing but want only to please and be pleased. You may be on your knees or laid out across the floor. It is a place where there is only pleasure. You know what to do, and what to say; if anything at all. Everything is gentle and loving and so wonderful... You just receive because it feels so very good and somehow you react with gestures that flow from you to Him and you know this is good. Healing flows here. Answers come in this place of WORSHIP. The Word of God is revealed to you here. This has got to be that secret place we are told to go to; to abide under the shadow of the Almighty. No one could tell you of this place with mere words through teaching. One must enter in and come to this place of WORSHIP.

When a man and a woman come together in marriage they are not as one until they have made love to one another. They come to know exactly where to touch and what to say that will bring satisfying pleasure to the other. They actually become one in love and pleasure along with the knowledge of how to please without physically touching. They grow together continually to a place where one or the other cannot take anymore. The desire has grown into a need to touch and be touched; to taste and be tasted. They explode in an ecstasy of… Ah, but this place is shared by the two of them alone. As in the marriage bed, no other is allowed, so is it in this place of WORSHIP.

Having such a loving relationship, they have an air about them that draws others to them. Others see the light of God on you. This place of ecstasy is the same as worship unto the Father; with Him, only He will not give you more than you can handle. The places you may touch are secret and special as are the places He touches with you. You can be in this place… if you choose to be. You can come to know this place and return again and again. He wants you to know Him as He knows you. Like a seed planted, with watering and proper care it will grow and multiply; so also will this relationship with the Father. **WORSHIP HIM!**

Rejoice!

YOU MAY STILL be in a place of song, yet feeling so very satisfied; wanting more now than ever to bring added pleasure to the Father. The pleasure you have given is nothing in comparison to what He has given you so you greatly desire to give more of yourself to Him; to do more of what He desires of you. You feel empty yet filled wondering where you can draw strength to give more but it is there; you can sense it deep inside slowly bubbling up to explode outward. You just know there is more to give. You are so happy, overjoyed. You may sing or clap; lift your hands or dance; cry and laugh; whisper or shout… You know that deep within you there is so very much more to this relationship. You have gotten here once and you can do it again. What you have experienced and learned can only be enhanced as you draw closer again. The relationship can only become richer and fuller. You know this place and have taken the steps to this explosion of joy. You will never forget this place of REJOICE. It is not the end for it is the beginning of something wonderful because you have been awakened. **REJOICE!**

Rejoice in the Lord always and again I say Rejoice.
—Philippians 4:4

Delight yourself in the Lord and He will give you the desires of your heart.
—Psalm 37:4

The Lord tells us to search the scriptures and in them we will find eternal life. *(John 5:39)* The Lord is warning His people that the fulfilling of scriptural prophecies are drawing near leaving us with Psalms which is praise and worship; intimate and experienced testimonials being shared with us; and Proverbs which are words of instruction. God is calling His people to a place of praise, bless, worship and rejoicing. It is a place of purity and truth. Not everyone will enter in because they do not understand the simplicity of God giving them a choice. The scriptures and Jesus are one *(John1:1, 14)* and Jesus continually points us to the Father. He even prays in *John 17* for us to be one in Him; although He pray for this, He will never force the choice to follow through on anyone.

In Matthew 15:8, 9 we can sense the displeasure as Jesus speaks: This people draws near with their mouths, and honor me with their lips; but their hearts are far from me. But in vain do they worship me, teaching for doctrines the commandments of men. We do not NEED buildings to have God dwell near us because He wants to dwell in each of us. The buildings are just places where we can come together in one accord. We are the Body of Christ and are given instruction by the Holy Spirit. We, each of us individually and together corporately, are the temple that must worship Him in Spirit and in Truth. He waits on us to choose each step of the way.

- Have you accepted Jesus as your Lord and Savior? No one can come to the Father except through Jesus.
- Have you received the infilling of the Holy Spirit? This is not a salvation issue but it is a relationship issue.
- Have you gone through a cleansing of the baptism of fire? This is all about understanding that sin separates us from God. He wants us to recognize the sin, admit to it, receive forgiveness of it and turn away from it; repentance.
- Are you at the gates of decision?
- Have you chosen to enter in? You cannot choose for someone else, only for yourself.

If the answer is "yes" to all of the questions above then I would say that you are well on your way to experiencing the fullness of the loving relationship God is calling you to with Him.

In the beginning, God...

Join the Father in pure worship; uniting with Him in an overpowering ecstasy of growth, learning, loving and pleasure that can only be found with Him; in Him. It is real and true. It is your choice. Unite and be one with the Father. Choose ye this day whom you will serve, yourself or Him.

In Him we live
And move
And have our being

In Him we live
And move
And have our being
(Acts 17:28)

Make a joyful noise
Sing unto the Lord
(Psalm 81:1)
(Psalm 98:4)
Tell Him of your love
Dance before Him
(Psalm 18:1)
(Psalm 150:4)

Psalm 100 Make a joyful noise unto the Lord, all ye lands. Serve the Lord with gladness: come before His presence with singing. Know ye that the Lord He is God: It is He that has made us, and not we ourselves; we are His people, and the sheep of His pasture. Enter into His gates with thanksgiving, and into His courts with praise: be thankful unto Him, and bless His name. For the Lord is good; His mercy is everlasting; and His truth endureth to all generations.

Abba Father
I want to thank you for the precious gift you have
given us in Jesus. I want to praise you for your
Word that we can glean understanding from it;
and come to know you more.
Thank you for teaching us, Father, how you feel
about us. Thank you for teaching us to
draw near to you
that you may draw near to us.
Holy Spirit, Continue doing a work in and through
us. Jesus helps us remember that you made a
way & are the only way to the Father.
Father help us to know you more, not just read
about it. Help us to walk securely, daily in this
new light, fully knowing that we can bring our
sisters to birth into our beautiful family
while basking in your presence.
Thank you, Father.
In Jesus Name
Amen

Printed in the United States
138700LV00001B/28/P

9 781414 113272